Benoit Tranquille Berbiguier
18 STUDIES FOR FLUTE

Edited by Carol Wincenc

Contents

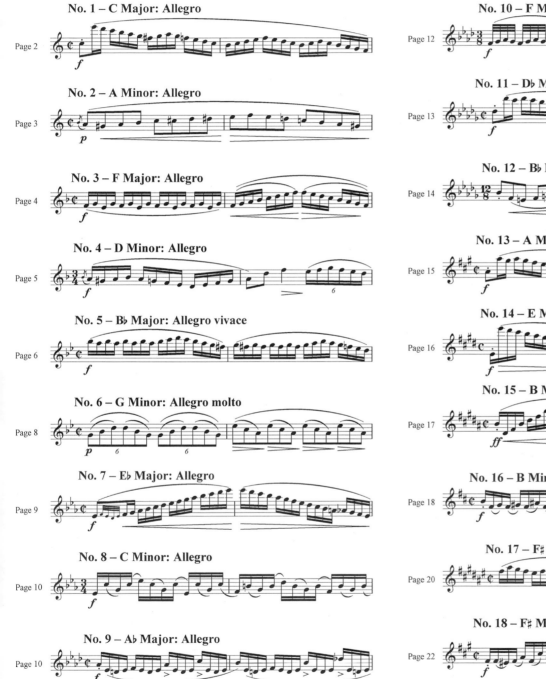

Page 2 — No. 1 – C Major: Allegro

Page 3 — No. 2 – A Minor: Allegro

Page 4 — No. 3 – F Major: Allegro

Page 5 — No. 4 – D Minor: Allegro

Page 6 — No. 5 – B♭ Major: Allegro vivace

Page 8 — No. 6 – G Minor: Allegro molto

Page 9 — No. 7 – E♭ Major: Allegro

Page 10 — No. 8 – C Minor: Allegro

Page 10 — No. 9 – A♭ Major: Allegro

Page 12 — No. 10 – F Minor: Moderato

Page 13 — No. 11 – D♭ Major: Allegro

Page 14 — No. 12 – B♭ Minor: Prestissimo

Page 15 — No. 13 – A Major: Allegro

Page 16 — No. 14 – E Major: Allegro

Page 17 — No. 15 – B Major: Allegro

Page 18 — No. 16 – B Minor: Moderato

Page 20 — No. 17 – F♯ Major: Allegro

Page 22 — No. 18 – F♯ Minor: Allegro non troppo

EIGHTEEN EXERCISES OR ETUDES
for Flute

Edited by Carol Wincenc and Bryan Wagorn

BENOIT TRANQUILLE BERBIGUIER
(1782–1835)

No. 1 – C Major
Allegro

No. 2 – A Minor

Allegro

* Flute composers of Berbiguier's period used the indication **tr** for all kinds of ornaments. Practice as a conventional, standard trill starting *on* the trill note, as well as the usual *Gruppetto*, to be executed thusly:

No. 3 – F Major

Allegro

No. 4 – D Minor

Allegro

6

No. 5 – B♭ Major
Allegro vivace

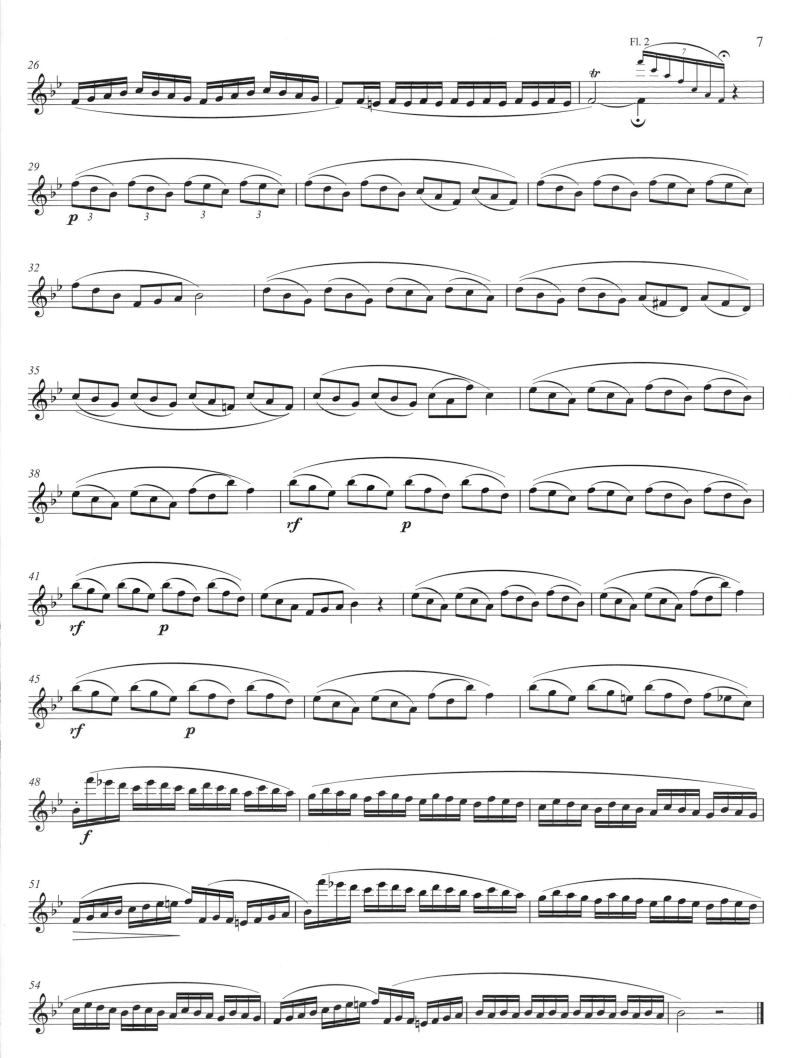

No. 6 – G Minor
Allegro molto

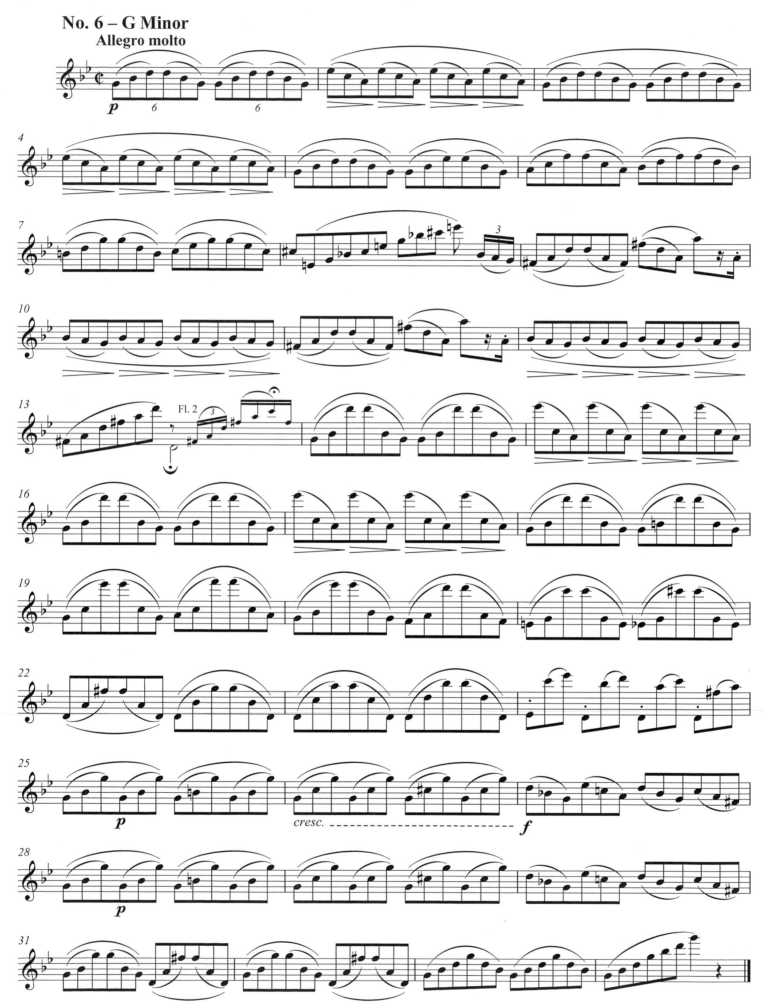

No. 7 – E♭ Major

Allegro

(an alternative)

10

No. 8 – C Minor
Allegro

No. 9 – A♭ Major
Allegro

No. 10 – F Minor
Moderato

Benoit Tranquille Berbiguier
18 STUDIES FOR FLUTE

Flute II
Composed by Carol Wincenc

Contents

No. 1 – C Major: Allegro — Page 4

No. 2 – A Minor: Allegro — Page 4

No. 3 – F Major: Allegro — Page 5

No. 4 – D Minor: Allegro — Page 6

No. 5 – B♭ Major: Allegro vivace — Page 6

No. 6 – G Minor: Allegro molto — Page 7

No. 7 – E♭ Major: Allegro — Page 8

No. 8 – C Minor: Allegro — Page 8

No. 9 – A♭ Major: Allegro — Page 9

No. 10 – F Minor: Moderato — Page 10

No. 11 – D♭ Major: Allegro — Page 10

No. 12 – B♭ Minor: Prestissimo — Page 11

No. 13 – A Major: Allegro — Page 12

No. 14 – E Major: Allegro — Page 12

No. 15 – B Major: Allegro — Page 13

No. 16 – B Minor: Allegro — Page 14

No. 17 – F♯ Major: Allegro — Page 15

No. 18 – F♯ Minor: Allegro non troppo — Page 16

2

Benoit Tranquille Berbiguier (1782-1838) was a renowned French flutist. Clearly a man who loved the instrument, his "Nouvelle Methode Pour la Flute" (dated 1818), nearly 300 pages long, is a virtual encyclopedia of flute playing and contains fingering diagrams, explanation of Italian musical terms, trill and ornament charts, advice on how to practice, and numerous studies and musical examples designed to build technique. Also included are the 18 Studies which we present here. Among his most often-played pieces, they are recognized for their musical as well as pedagogical value, and are an important part of any flutist's training. Do not be deceived by the seemingly "elementary" appearance of both the Flute 1 and Flute 2 parts. In the words of Ms Wincenc: "There are plenty of finger twisters throughout many of them. And as my esteemed colleague and 'other' French mentor, Jean-Pierre Rampal, used to say, 'Oooh La La! You can REALLY break your leg on theees one.'"

The idea of creating a second flute part has its foundation in the teachings of the great French flutist Marcel Moyse (a pivotal mentor to Professor Wincenc). In lessons, Moyse would accompany the student on his own instrument, and often vocally improvise melodies and/or lyrics. In adding his second line, Moyse was able to underscore the harmonic, melodic, rhythmic structure and shape of the lines in a way which went far beyond any possible verbal explanation. This way, the student learned about rhythmic stability, phrasing, intonation, and quality of sound by playing with the master.

After an initial playthrough of the first few etudes, we were puzzled by the significant discrepancies between the different editions of the work. Inconsistencies in dynamics, notes, time signatures, and even the length of etudes left us unsure of how to arrive at an authoritative edition. Through the generosity of the New York Public Library for the Performing Arts, we were able to consult an original edition of the Method, housed in its Special Collection. Thus we were able to solve the mystery of the various editions, and while ours enriches the original with dynamics and articulation markings to help guide the student to an expressive and sensitive interpretation, the text on the whole keeps closely with Berbiguier's original. Of particular interest was Berbiguier's frequent use of cut time rather than common time, and his use of Rinforzando instead of Sforzando (the former indicating a "reinforcement" of a note, rather than an application of a sudden, strong accent).

The prominent 19th century flutist Henri Altes also created a second flute part to these etudes. It was rewarding to see that such an important figure in the history of the flute found pedagogical value in creating a second flute part as well.

We hope that by offering our second flute part, students and teachers will get even more out of Berbiguier's studies. The student will be required to attend to several issues, including breath, intonation, and ensemble. Learning how to breathe quickly in a way which does not disrupt either the melodic line or the ensemble with the other flute part is a practiced skill and must be planned in advance while working alone on the etude. When playing together, careful attention to intonation and the quality of your sound will develop the skills required of an outstanding flutist and of a sensitive chamber musician and collaborator.

Carol Wincenc, Composer and Editor
Bryan Wagorn, Assistant Composer and Editor
New York City
July 2012

Carol Wincenc 21st Century Series for Flute

Grammy and recent National Flute Association Lifetime Achievement Award winner, flutist Carol Wincenc celebrated her 2010 Ruby Anniversary with rave reviews from the New York Times, Wall Street Journal, The New Yorker, and Performance Today. Beloved muse of today's most prominent composers, she has premiered concerti written for her by Lukas Foss, Henryk Gorecki, Joan Tower, Paul Schoenfield, Jake Heggie, Peter Schickele, Roberto Sierra and Tobias Picker. A prolific recording artist, her performance of Pulitzer Prize winner Christopher Rouse's Flute Concerto with the Houston Symphony on Telarc Records won her the coveted Diapason d'Or Award, and her recording with Maestro Jo Ann Falletta and the Buffalo Philharmonic on Naxos was Gramophone's Pick of the Month. As winner of the sole Walter W. Naumburg Solo Flute Competition she recorded a disc of French music with pianist Andras Schiff on the Music Masters label, which was awarded the Recording of Special Merit.

She has appeared as soloist with such luminary ensembles as the Chicago, St. Louis, San Francisco, Detroit, Pittsburgh, Atlanta, BBC, Warsaw, and London Symphonies, and the St. Paul, Mostly Mozart, Los Angeles, and English Chamber Orchestras. She has performed at music festivals in Aldeburgh, Budapest, Frankfurt, Santa Fe, Spoleto, Banff, Sarasota, Music@Menlo, Norfolk, Tivoli and Marlboro. A founding member of her Trio Les Amies with New York Philharmonic principals, harpist Nancy Allen and violist Cynthia Phelps, she is also a longtime member of the prestigious New York Woodwind Quintet. Her recording of the Mozart Flute Quartets on Deutsche Grammophon with the Emerson String Quartet is regarded as one of the definitive interpretations of these works.

As a result of her fascination with the flute family, Wincenc created and directed a series of International Flute Festivals in St. Paul, Minnesota, featuring such diverse artists as Jean-Pierre Rampal, Herbie Mann, and Native American flutist R. Carlos Nakai. Lauren Keiser Music Publishing and Carl Fischer publish a series of Carol Wincenc Signature Editions, featuring her favorite flute repertoire. Ms. Wincenc continues her teaching legacy at Stony Brook University as well as her alma mater, The Juilliard School, graduating masterful students holding prominent careers worldwide as teachers, concerto soloists, and orchestral musicians.

These new editions are thoroughly edited with modern new engravings utilizing a spread out, easy to read format, upscale paper and an affordable price for the value. She comments on the music and gives priceless advice and performance suggestions.

M. A. Reichert *Seven Daily Exercises for Flute, Op. 5*, a flutist's "bible" for warm-ups are presented in a new edition with wide spaced notation and meticulous editing. **HL00042281**

Ernesto Kohler *35 Exercises for Flute, Op. 33, Books 1 &2* These classic, standard etudes are presented in a new edition with fine re-engraved music, performance suggestions and Ms. Wincenc's articulated comments.
   Book 1: **HL00042282**
   Book 2: **HL00042283**

Joachim Andersen *Twenty-Four Etudes for Flute, Op. 15 with Flute 2 part* immortalizes Ms. Wincenc's inspiring sessions with the great French flutist Marcel Moyse by creating a second flute part playable by the teacher or a fellow student. This unique approach underscores the musical elements within the lines and teaches the student rhythmic stability, phrasing, intonation, and quality of sound. The edition also offers a unique glimpse into Andersen's brilliance and creativity with his included manuscript fragment and sketch from Etude Op. 15 No. 1. **HL00042675**

18 Studies for Flute by Renowned French flutist Benoit Tranquille Berbiguier (1782-1838) are among his most often-played pieces, recognized for their musical as well as pedagogical value, and are an important part of any flutist's training. This is a new Urtext edition with a Flute 2 part composed by Carol Wincenc, based on the methods of one of her most pivotal influences, the great flutist Marcel Moyse. **HL00109366**

LAUREN KEISER MUSIC PUBLISHING

Exclusively Distributed By
HAL•LEONARD®

Trade/Dealer Sales
1-800-554-0626
(fax) 1-414-774-3259
sales@halleonard.com

Consumer Credit Card Orders
1-800-637-2852

International Accounts
1-414-774-3630
(fax) 1-414-774-3259
sales@halleonard.com

Contact Us/Questions?
info@laurenkeisermusic.com

EIGHTEEN EXERCISES OR ETUDES
for Flute

Composed and Edited by
CAROL WINCENC and
BRYAN WAGORN

No. 1 – C Major
Allegro

No. 2 – A Minor
Allegro

* Flute composers of Berbiguier's period used the indication *tr* for all kinds of ornaments. Practice as a conventional, standard trill starting *on* the trill note, as well as the usual *Gruppetto*, to be executed thusly:

No. 3 – F Major
Allegro

No. 6 – G Minor
Allegro molto

No. 7 – E♭ Major

Allegro vivace

No. 8 – C Minor

Allegro

(2nd time *p*)

No. 9 – A♭ Major
Allegro

No. 12 – Bb Minor
Prestissimo

No. 13 – A Major

Allegro

No. 14 – E Major

Allegro

No. 15 – B Major
Allegro

No. 16 – B Minor

* In Berbiguier's first edition, *senza tempo* referred to mm. 49–52, where Berbiguier did not enter any bar lines. For the sake of clarity, our edition has this passage measured into complete bars. Nevertheless, both Flutes 1 and 2 may be played freely.

No. 17 – F# Major
Allegro

No. 18 – F# Minor
Allegro non troppo

No. 11 – D♭ Major

Allegro

No. 12 – B♭ Minor

Prestissimo

No. 13 – A Major
Allegro

Also practice as a conventional, standard trill.

16

No. 14 – E Major
Allegro

No. 15 – B Major
Allegro

Also practice as a conventional, standard trill.

No. 16 – B Minor
Moderato

* In Berbiguier's first edition, *senza tempo* referred to mm. 49–52, where Berbiguier did not enter any bar lines. For the sake of
clarity, our edition has this passage measured into complete bars. Nevertheless, both Flutes 1 and 2 may be played freely.

20

No. 17 – F♯ Major
Allegro

No. 18 – F♯ Minor

Allegro non troppo

Carol Wincenc 21st Century Series for Flute

Grammy and recent National Flute Association Lifetime Achievement Award winner, flutist Carol Wincenc celebrated her 2010 Ruby Anniversary with rave reviews from the New York Times, Wall Street Journal, The New Yorker, and Performance Today. Beloved muse of today's most prominent composers, she has premiered concerti written for her by Lukas Foss, Henryk Gorecki, Joan Tower, Paul Schoenfield, Jake Heggie, Peter Schickele, Roberto Sierra and Tobias Picker. A prolific recording artist, her performance of Pulitzer Prize winner Christopher Rouse's Flute Concerto with the Houston Symphony on Telarc Records won her the coveted Diapason d'Or Award, and her recording with Maestro Jo Ann Falletta and the Buffalo Philharmonic on Naxos was Gramophone's Pick of the Month. As winner of the sole Walter W. Naumburg Solo Flute Competition she recorded a disc of French music with pianist Andras Schiff on the Music Masters label, which was awarded the Recording of Special Merit.

She has appeared as soloist with such luminary ensembles as the Chicago, St. Louis, San Francisco, Detroit, Pittsburgh, Atlanta, BBC, Warsaw, and London Symphonies, and the St. Paul, Mostly Mozart, Los Angeles, and English Chamber Orchestras. She has performed at music festivals in Aldeburgh, Budapest, Frankfurt, Santa Fe, Spoleto, Banff, Sarasota, Music@Menlo, Norfolk, Tivoli and Marlboro. A founding member of her Trio Les Amies with New York Philharmonic principals, harpist Nancy Allen and violist Cynthia Phelps, she is also a longtime member of the prestigious New York Woodwind Quintet. Her recording of the Mozart Flute Quartets on Deutsche Grammophon with the Emerson String Quartet is regarded as one of the definitive interpretations of these works.

As a result of her fascination with the flute family, Wincenc created and directed a series of International Flute Festivals in St. Paul, Minnesota, featuring such diverse artists as Jean-Pierre Rampal, Herbie Mann, and Native American flutist R. Carlos Nakai. Lauren Keiser Music Publishing and Carl Fischer publish a series of Carol Wincenc Signature Editions, featuring her favorite flute repertoire. Ms. Wincenc continues her teaching legacy at Stony Brook University as well as her alma mater, The Juilliard School, graduating masterful students holding prominent careers worldwide as teachers, concerto soloists, and orchestral musicians.

These new editions are thoroughly edited with modern new engravings utilizing a spread out, easy to read format, upscale paper and an affordable price for the value. She comments on the music and gives priceless advice and performance suggestions.

M. A. Reichert *Seven Daily Exercises for Flute, Op. 5*, a flutist's "bible" for warm-ups are presented in a new edition with wide spaced notation and meticulous editing. **HL00042281**

Ernesto Kohler 35 *Exercises for Flute, Op. 33, Books 1 &2* These classic, standard etudes are presented in a new edition with fine re-engraved music, performance suggestions and Ms. Wincenc's articulated comments.
Book 1: HL00042282
Book 2: HL00042283

Joachim Andersen *Twenty-Four Etudes for Flute, Op. 15 with Flute 2 part* immortalizes Ms. Wincenc's inspiring sessions with the great French flutist Marcel Moyse by creating a second flute part playable by the teacher or a fellow student. This unique approach underscores the musical elements within the lines and teaches the student rhythmic stability, phrasing, intonation, and quality of sound. The edition also offers a unique glimpse into Andersen's brilliance and creativity with his included manuscript fragment and sketch from Etude Op. 15 No. 1. **HL00042675**

18 Studies for Flute by Renowned French flutist Benoit Tranquille Berbiguier (1782-1838) are among his most often-played pieces, recognized for their musical as well as pedagogical value, and are an important part of any flutist's training. This is a new Urtext edition with a Flute 2 part composed by Carol Wincenc, based on the methods of one of her most pivotal influences, the great flutist Marcel Moyse. **HL00109366**

LAUREN KEISER **LK** MUSIC PUBLISHING

Exclusively Distributed By

HAL•LEONARD®

Trade/Dealer Sales
1-800-554-0626
(fax) 1-414-774-3259
sales@halleonard.com

Consumer Credit Card Orders
1-800-637-2852

International Accounts
1-414-774-3630
(fax) 1-414-774-3259
sales@halleonard.com

Contact Us/Questions?
info@laurenkeisermusic.com